BATHROOMS
Through the Ages

Richard Wood

WAYLAND

Editor: Jason Hook
Book design: Tony Truscott
Series design: Ian Winton
Cover design: Joyce Chester
Cartoon artwork: Tony de Saulles

This edition published in 2000 by Wayland Publishers Ltd

First published in 1999 by Wayland Publishers Ltd, 61 Western Road, Hove,
East Sussex, BN3 1JD, England

Find Wayland on the Internet at http://www.wayland.co.uk

British Library Cataloguing in Publication Data
Wood, Richard, 1949-
Bathrooms. - (Through the ages)
1. Bathrooms - History - Juvenile literature 2. Hygiene -
History - Juvenile literature
I. Title II. De Saulles, Tony
643.5'2'09

ISBN 0 7502 2629 3

Printed and bound by G. Canale & C. SpA, Turin, Italy

Cover picture: A knight in his bath attended by ladies, c. 1310–1340.
Title page: The death of Jean-Paul Marat in his bath, painted by David, c. 1793.

Picture Acknowledgements: The publishers would like to thank the following for permission to reproduce their pictures: AKG, London *cover* (main picture), 7, 11 (bottom), 13 (top), 16 (bottom), 17 (top), /Erich Lessing 5 (bottom), 6 (top), 8 (top), /John Hios 6 (bottom); Arcaid /Richard Bryant 19 (bottom), /Lucinda Lambton 25 (top), /John Edward Linden 29 (bottom); Bridgeman Art Library, London /Musée Conde, Chantilly, France /Giraudon 14 (top), /British Library, London 15 (top), /Musée National du Moyen Ages et des Thermes de Cluny, Paris /Peter Willi 18 (top), /Musée D'Orsay, Paris /Giraudon 24 (top); Chatsworth Photo Library 21 (top); C. M. Dixon 16 (top); Mary Evans 17 (bottom), 27 (bottom); Robert Harding 9 (right), 20 (bottom), 27 (top), /A. Woolfitt 8 (bottom), /Rolf Richardson 12; Museum of London 10–11 (top); National Portrait Gallery, London 20 (top); Natural History Museum, London 15 (bottom); Popperfoto 28; Public Record Office 29 (top); Royal Pavilion Libraries and Museums, Brighton 23 (bottom); Science Museum /Science and Society Picture Library 13 (bottom), 18 (bottom), 22 (top), 26 (top), 26 (bottom); Stock Market *cover* (background); Tony Stone /Erica Lansner 4 (top); Topham 5 (top), 10 (bottom); Wayland Picture Library 19 (top), 23 (top), 24 (bottom), /Zul Mukhida 25 (bottom); Richard Wood 4 (bottom).

CONTENTS

Ancient Ablutions

Down by the Riverside

How did our prehistoric ancestors keep clean? Did they scrape their bodies with sticks, or pour water over themselves? We know that prehistoric people often lived near rivers. We can guess that after a hot day's hunting, they cleaned themselves in the water. They probably found that bathing was fun as well as being healthy. No doubt some of them cleared bushes and stones away from their best bathing places. The first open-air bathrooms had come into being.

▶ The River Dordogne, in France. Prehistoric people drew paintings in nearby caves, and must have bathed here.

Speech Bubbles

Holy Soap
'"Although you wash yourself with soda and use an abundance of soap, the stain of your guilt is still before me," says the Lord.'
(Jeremiah 2: 22)

Cretan Comforts

The oldest indoor bathrooms were built at Mohenjo-Daro, India, in about 2500 BC. But the most splendid were at Knossos, in Crete. The Queen's Bath at Knossos dates from 1450 BC. The terracotta tub, shaped like a modern bath, stood in a beautiful bathroom decorated with dolphins. Slaves brought hot water in jugs, and the bath emptied through clay pipes. What luxury!

▶ The Queen's Bath at Knossos has a plughole and a stone plug.

Pharaoh Liquid

The ancient Egyptians did not have elaborate bathrooms. In the Bible, Moses finds the Pharaoh taking his morning bath in the River Nile, and this seems to have been normal for men. Women washed at home, but their baths were little more than shallow trays. Paintings on walls show bathing women kneeling while slaves pour water over them. Water was precious in the dry climate, and the Egyptians would have thought it very wasteful to fill up a deep tub.

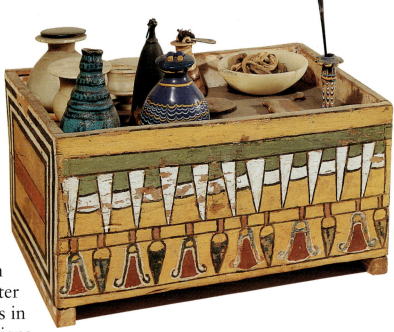

▲ This toilet box contained scrapers, cloths, perfumes and cosmetics. It belonged to a rich Egyptian woman in about 1420 BC.

FANCY THAT!

Milk Maiden
The Egyptian queen Cleopatra bathed in asses' milk. When the film Anthony and Cleopatra *was made in the 1930s, the actress Claudette Colbert insisted on having real asses' milk too!*

Bubble Trouble

It is hard to imagine taking a bath today without lots of soap to help clean away the dirt. In ancient times, soap was rare, though plants were sometimes used to make a lather. Soap is even mentioned in the Bible.

Proper soap was probably introduced to the Mediterranean countries by Phoenician traders about 2,500 years ago. They made it from goats' fat and the ashes of beech wood. Unfortunately it was very harsh and tended to burn the skin. The Roman writer Pliny says that the Celts in Britain also made soap this way, but they used it only to brighten their hair.

◄ This deep terracotta bath was used by the Hittites, whose Asian kingdom lasted from 1600 to 1200 BC.

Grubby Greeks

Gym Slips

In ancient Greece, men and boys lived an athletic life. They spent part of every day exercising or competing in games in the sports arena. The word 'gymnasium' comes from a Greek word which means 'to exercise naked'. Next to every Greek gym there was a public bath. Once they had worked up a sweat in the arena, the athletes slipped into the bath to cool down and get clean.

The gymnasium bath was always cold. Greek doctors such as Hippocrates said cold baths were a cure for most illnesses. Greek men disliked hot baths. The writer Hesiod said that they were suitable only for women.

▲ A Greek athlete cleans himself with a strigil. The picture comes from the side of an oil pot.

► This metal strigil comes from the baths at Olympia, where the ancient Olympic Games were held.

Speech Bubbles

Rub-a-Dub
'Telemachus and Peisistratos went to the polished bath tubs and bathed; or rather, the house-maidens bathed them and rubbed them down with oil.'
(*The Odyssey*, Homer, c. 700 BC)

Well Oiled

Unlike the Phoenicians, the Greeks did not use soap. Instead, they first took a bath and dried themselves. Then they rubbed olive oil into their skin. Once this had absorbed all the sweat and dirt, they scraped it off with metal scrapers called 'strigils'. This left them feeling fresh, tingling and very clean. Rich Greeks employed slaves to scrape them, but friends often scraped each other.

Eureka!

When Archimedes, the Greek scientist, climbed into a full bath he spilled some water over the side. This made him realize that the weight of the spilled water would be the same as that lost by his own body when in water. He was so excited that he jumped out of his bath and ran naked down the street shouting 'Eureka!' – which means 'I have found it!' We call this important discovery 'Archimedes' Principle'.

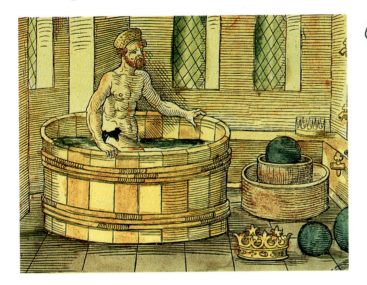

FANCY THAT!

Blood Bath
After capturing Troy, the Greek hero Agamemnon returned home to his wife. Apparently, she was not pleased to see him. She waited until he was in the bath, then struck him twice with an axe and killed him.

◀ Archimedes (287–212 BC), who discovered something important in his bath.

Tanked Up

Cleanliness was important to the Greeks. As well as using the gymnasium baths, many families had bathrooms in their own homes. These usually had shallow ceramic or metal baths, but a few lucky people had deep tubs. The Greeks collected rainwater in tanks on their roofs and piped it directly to the bath, sometimes through an overhead shower. It was good manners in ancient Greece always to offer a bath to a newly arrived guest. Warm water was permitted for women, who liked to splash themselves with perfume after a hot bath.

▲ A Greek woman with a washbasin and mirror, pictured on a fifth-century cup.

The Public Plunge

A Healthy Mind

We take a bath in order to wash. But the ancient Romans took a bath to be healthy rather than just to be clean. Our word 'sanitation' reminds us of pipes, plumbers and drains. But it comes from the Roman word 'sanitas', which means health. The Romans had a saying, *mens sana in sana corporis*, which means 'a healthy mind in a healthy body'. They believed a bath was the best way to achieve both.

▶ This fourth-century mosaic from Piazza Armerina, Sicily, shows a Roman woman wearing a bikini.

Crazy Bathing

The first Roman public baths were mainly used by poor people. However, by AD 50 the rich had caught the bathing craze. Public baths became social clubs where important Romans went to meet their friends. By AD 300, Rome had eleven huge public baths, equipped with gyms, restrooms, libraries and restaurants. Public toilets were often just outside, and were flushed with dirty bathwater every time the baths were emptied. You can imagine how much water the Romans used.

◀ The Roman water supply at Bath. A Roman town-dweller used six times as much water as a modern Londoner.

Roman Roaming

Roman baths had a courtyard at their centre, where people exercised before bathing. Round this courtyard were several pools at different temperatures. Bathers began in cold water, then went to a warm bath. Next, they took a steam bath in the *sudatorium*. Then, after sweating here for as long as they could stand it, they plunged back into the cold bath to finish.

◀ Women beat each other with branches to open the pores of the skin before they took a bath.

▲ The Great Bath at Bath, Somerset, is still fed by naturally hot springs. The Romans called it *Aquae Sulis* after Sulis, the goddess of health.

Mix and Match

The Romans usually bathed naked, so men and women did not bathe together. Some baths had separate male and female sections. Others used the same baths but at different times of the day. Bells were rung to signal changeover times. From about AD 350, mixed bathing was allowed in many baths, and they became popular places for men and women to meet. Respectable girls now stayed away.

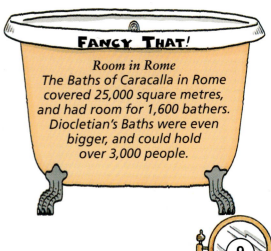

FANCY THAT!

Room in Rome
The Baths of Caracalla in Rome covered 25,000 square metres, and had room for 1,600 bathers. Diocletian's Baths were even bigger, and could hold over 3,000 people.

Private Pleasures

Villa Filler

Public baths became so popular with the Romans that few people in towns had bathrooms at home. But in the country, with no public baths nearby, rich Romans had to build their own. Just like the public baths, the country villas had different baths filled with cold, warm and hot water, each in a separate room. Some villas had a second set of baths, perhaps for use by the slaves. Special implements were used in these luxurious villa bathrooms, to keep every part of the body clean.

▶ A Roman bather's tweezers (left) for plucking hair, and an ear-cleaner (right) called a *ligula*.

FANCY THAT!

Dinner Dips
Most Romans preferred to take a bath before dinner. Sometimes they took another bath after the meal, to restore their appetite so that they could begin eating all over again.

Furnace Features

Baths were heated by hot air from a furnace, which was blown beneath the villa floors. It went first to the sweat room, then on to the cooler rooms. This clever underfloor heating system was called the *hypocaust*. To prevent fire from spreading if there was an accident, bathrooms were usually built well away from the living quarters.

◀ Remains of a hypocaust at Fishbourne Roman Villa, in Sussex.

A Good Scrape

Like the Greeks, the Romans used oil and strigils to clean their bodies. The olive oil they used was very expensive in Britain, as it had to be imported from Spain or Italy. If they were very dirty, bathers mixed sand with the oil and rubbed it well into the skin. Scraping it off again must have been very painful.

▲ Romans used this strigil and manicure set during their long hours spent in the different baths.

Water Sports

Not all Romans bathed every day, but when they did they set aside an hour or two to enjoy it to the full. There were special sports, such as handball, to play in the water. Gambling and board games were enjoyed in the steamy atmosphere of the hot room. Meals were even served on floating trays.

▶ Bathroom floors were decorated with mosaics of watery scenes, such as this goddess bathing with her nymphs.

Dark-Age Dips

Soap and Pillage

When the Roman Empire ended in about AD 410, public bathhouses closed and people lost interest in regular bathing. The Saxons did not have bathrooms, and they despised people who were too clean. But the Vikings, who raided and pillaged across Europe in the 800s, were very different. They changed their clothes regularly, combed their hair every day, and even took a bath on Saturdays. We should not be surprised that the Vikings enjoyed a dip. After all, their homes were surrounded by the beautiful waters of Scandinavia's many fjords.

SPEECH BUBBLES

Mucky Monks
'To the monks that are well, and especially to the young, shall bathing seldom be permitted.' (Rule of St Benedict, about AD 540)

▼ The watery landscape of Scandinavia, where the Vikings enjoyed a regular bath.

▼ Mixed bathing, which was banned by the Church.

Sins of the Bather

You might think that the Church encouraged clean habits. In fact, religious leaders saw dirtiness as a sign of holiness. They believed that suffering of any sort – including the suffering of being very dirty – could help bring people closer to God. But there was another reason why the Church tried to discourage bathing. Baths were usually shared, sometimes by men and women together. St Boniface thought this was sinful, and banned mixed bathing in AD 745.

▼ This illustration of the soapwort plant comes from a sixth-century book about useful herbs.

FANCY THAT!

High and Holy
When St Agnes died at the age of thirteen, it was said that she had never taken a bath, or even washed. People said this showed how holy she was.

Soap and Sap

In Europe in the 1100s, professional soap-makers went into business. But poor people could not afford soap and the rich did not want it, so it was not a popular luxury. In Norman Britain, some people used soapwort instead. The sap of this plant makes a lather and helps to dissolve dirt. People also used flower petals and leaves to scent their bathwater.

Holy Water

▲ A baptism scene painted in about 1370. The font is a miniature stone bath filled with holy water.

An Early Bath

Medieval babies were baptized when they were just a few days old. Baptism made the new baby a full member of the Christian Church. Unlike today, babies were not just sprinkled with a few drops of water. Instead, the priest dunked them in the font, dipping them completely under the water three times. Fonts had to be kept locked to stop people stealing the holy water, which was thought by some to have magical properties.

FANCY THAT!

Saints and Sinners
Cold water was used for baptism, to wash away a baby's sins. Hot water, when used in adults' baths, was thought to be a sinful luxury.

Laver Louts

Monks were probably the cleanest people in medieval times. Monasteries were normally built next to rivers, so there was always plenty of fresh water. Baths were permitted only for sick monks, and even they were allowed only cold water. Running water was piped instead to basins called 'lavers', where the monks could wash before meals. There were bathroom rules ordering the monks not to 'blow their noses on the towels or remove dirt with them.'

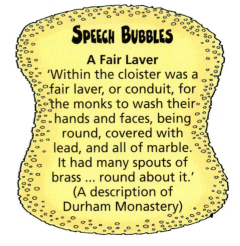

SPEECH BUBBLES

A Fair Laver
'Within the cloister was a fair laver, or conduit, for the monks to wash their hands and faces, being round, covered with lead, and all of marble. It had many spouts of brass ... round about it.'
(A description of Durham Monastery)

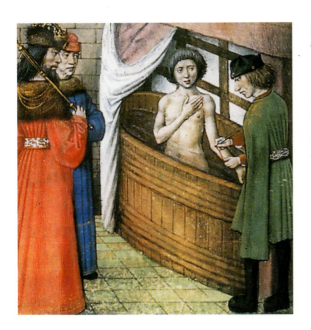

Bath Robes

The hot springs at Bath in Somerset had been forgotten since Roman times. But in the 1100s, the old Roman bath was reopened. People began to bathe there again, to improve their health. It was said that the waters could cure 'leprosy, pocks, scabs and great aches'. After seeing many naked bodies at Bath, in 1449 the local bishop ordered every bather over thirteen years of age to wear drawers or a robe.

◀ Baths have often been used as health cures. This bather is having blood removed, to try to cure a disease.

Bad Hair Day

Medieval people rarely, if ever, washed their hair. Consequently, hair often became infested with many creepy-crawlies. It was considered bad manners to take off your hat at mealtimes, in case headlice dropped into the food. People sometimes rinsed their hair with a mixture of beaten eggs, lemon juice, vinegar and white wine, just to stop their heads itching.

▶ A woman using a stiff brush to remove lice from a man's wet hair, pictured in a book from 1491.

Middle-Age Muck

Tale of the Tub

Medieval bath tubs were made of wood, and looked like big, oval-shaped barrels. A backrest stuck up at each end, containing a handle for carrying the bath. Tubs were lined with canvas, to make them watertight and prevent painful splinters. Large households had bathroom equipment which included tilting washbasins, towels on rollers and 'aquamanile' jugs shaped like animals.

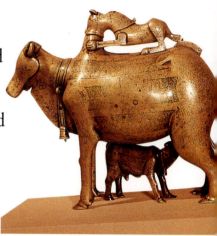

Rude to be Nude?

For medieval people, it was not always rude to be nude. The Church disapproved, of course. But men and women often bathed together at home, or even out of doors. Paintings show them playing dice or cards, listening to music, or eating elaborate meals from planks placed between them across the top of the tub.

▲ Aquamanile jugs were used for pouring water over the hands. This one, from Persia, is shaped like a cow.

◄ A couple in a steamy bath are served with a meal in a public bathhouse.

SPEECH BUBBLES

Water Torture
'They shut her in a bath and set alight,
A mighty fire beneath it.
Day and night,
They stoked it, and from night to day again.
Yet she sat cold and felt of it no pain.'
(Geoffrey Chaucer, *Second Nun's Tale*, c. 1380s)

Bath Knight

For medieval squires to become knights, it was not always enough just to win a few jousts. King Henry IV made new knights have a cold bath, too. Like a Christian baptism, the bath was a sign that the squire had washed away his old life, before starting afresh as a knight. Older knights poured water over the squire while teaching him his duties. He then became a 'Knight of the Bath'. The title is still used today – but not the bath.

▲ Beneath his helmet and shield, this painting shows a knight being attended in his bath.

FANCY THAT!

Royal Soaks
The first English bath with hot and cold running water was installed for King Edward III in 1351. Accounts show that the king bought two bronze taps from a man called Robert the Founder.

In a Stew

From the late 1300s, many public bathhouses were opened in European cities. They were known as 'hot houses' or 'stews', because the water was heated in big cauldrons, like a stew. There were eighteen stews on Stewsbank by the Thames in Southwark, London. Boys were sent through the streets every morning to shout out when the water was hot. Men and women bathed together in big tubs, and they could buy food and drink. Attendants called 'stovers' were on hand to shave bathers, cut their hair or even perform minor operations.

▶ These stews in Germany were used as a social club by the bathers.

Tudor Odours

A Steamy Story

In Tudor times, the new craze was the Turkish bath. Here, bathers sweated out their dirt in clouds of steam. Some baths were built next to bakeries, and used the steam from their ovens. Unfortunately, diseases like the plague were passed between bathers and in the 1530s Henry VIII had to close London's baths.

FANCY THAT!

Mixed Blessings
Leonardo da Vinci designed a mixer tap for the Queen of Spain's bathroom. It mixed three parts boiling water with one cold.

◀ Turkish baths were not the only luxury. Tudor nobles took over the monasteries' water systems to supply their own baths. This rich lady is bathing in her garden.

▼ This little silver case is called a pomander. The design on the side suggests that people sniffed it to protect them from the plague, which was spread by rats.

Pongs and Perfumes

Instead of washing themselves, many Tudors covered up foul body odours by carrying sweet-smelling pomanders and 'nosegays', or splashing their filthy bodies with scented water. Queen Elizabeth I liked to scent her body after bathing. She made her own perfumes from flower petals, and told all the ladies at court to keep perfumed boxes, called 'scented coffers', at their bedsides.

SPEECH BUBBLES

Foot Note

Many Tudor ladies cared very little about personal hygiene. When somebody told one grand lady, 'Your hands are filthy,' she replied, 'Then you should see my feet!'

Bathing Queens

Elizabeth I had the luxury of heated bathrooms at Windsor Castle, which were lined with mirrors. She said that she took a bath every month 'whether she needed it or no'. To her filthy subjects, this made Elizabeth an unusually clean queen. Mary, Queen of Scots, had her own ideas about baths. She sometimes bathed in wine to freshen her body.

▶ Mary, Queen of Scots, who liked a drink in her bath, and to bath in her drink.

High Society

While the rich and royal bathed, the poor remained unwashed. Their streets and homes were so filthy they probably did not notice how smelly their own bodies were. The water supply in most towns was so poor that people did not have enough water to fill a bath, even if they wanted to.

Bad breath was as big a problem as body odours. Toothbrushes are not mentioned until 1651. Instead, some people used their urine as a mouthwash. Others cleaned their teeth with mallow roots, charcoal or soot. Even Queen Elizabeth's teeth eventually turned completely black.

◀ Only the rich had beautiful bathrooms like this one in Florence, Italy.

Laps of Luxury

Soap Opera

There were some dirty tactics in the English Civil War, which was fought between the king and parliament. In 1638, King Charles I tried to raise money for his army by charging people for permission to make soap. So, most soap-makers supported parliament. But after the king's death in 1649, things got even worse for the soap-makers. The new ruler, Oliver Cromwell, now introduced a heavy tax on soap.

◀ Oliver Cromwell ruled England from 1649 to 1658.

The Barber of Cologne

What better than a good splash of eau de Cologne after a hot bath? This famous toilet water got its name because it was invented in Cologne, Germany, by a barber, in the early 1600s. He made it from the oil of lemons and oranges, which he mixed with lavender water and orange blossom. This art of taking the scent of flowers and dissolving it in fats or oils is called 'enfleurage'. Men and women loved to soak up their favourite scents by adding perfume to their nice, hot bathwater.

▶ This seventeenth-century scent bottle held toilet water to use after bathing.

French Fashions

A French fashion for luxury bathrooms was copied by British lords and ladies. In 1692, the Duke of Devonshire had a marble grotto built at Chatsworth House in Derbyshire. It had statues, fountains and a bath big enough for two. Lord Bacon installed two 'bathing rooms' at his home in Hertfordshire. In his book *Instructions for Taking a Bath*, he wrote: 'First rub the body with oil ... then sit two hours in the bath. After bathing, wrap the body in a cloth ... until the body be grown solid and hard.'

Speech Bubbles

A Clean Resolution
'My wife [went] to the hot house to bathe herself. She now pretends to a resolution of being hereafter very clean. How long it will hold I can guess.'
(Diary of Samuel Pepys, 1660s)

▲ The grotto at Chatsworth is decorated with sea creatures and a figure of the goddess Diana bathing.

Bed Baths

Every great French house had a suite of baths. King Louis XIV's palace at Versailles had a hundred bathrooms, each with giant marble baths and bronze taps. But the baths were rather hard and cold, so the king preferred to bathe in a wooden tub in his bedroom. When he did use a marble bath, the sides were draped with lace-trimmed cloths, and cushions were provided for him to sit on.

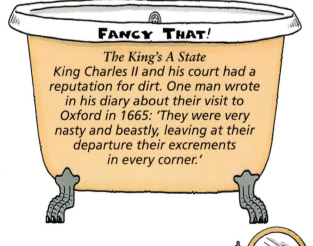

Fancy That!

The King's A State
King Charles II and his court had a reputation for dirt. One man wrote in his diary about their visit to Oxford in 1665: 'They were very nasty and beastly, leaving at their departure their excrements in every corner.'

21

Bidets and Bathdays

The Science of Appliance

A daily wash of the hands and face was fashionable in the 1700s. Furniture-makers turned their tools to appliances for bathrooms, and washing cabinets for bedrooms. There were washstands with china jugs and bowls, shaving tables with mirrors, and 'night tables' containing 'bidets'. The bidet was introduced from France. It was a shallow bath about the size and shape of a violin case, and was used for washing the private parts. Soldiers could buy shockproof bidets with removable legs, for use in wartime.

Taking the Plunge

Cold baths were popular again, but more for health than cleanliness. Doctors claimed that a regular cold bath could strengthen the body and cure headaches and 'vapours'. Many owners of country houses installed bathrooms with plunge baths. These were like small swimming pools, and were usually built in the basement, or in a building in the garden.

▲ This device is a gentleman's travelling case, with everything necessary for washing and shaving, used in the 1800s.

FANCY THAT!

Water Loo
The English general Wellington took a cold bath every morning. But the French leader Napoleon preferred his daily bath very hot. Perhaps the Battle of Waterloo was won in the bathroom, not on the battlefield.

SPEECH BUBBLES

Grime Report
'Most men resident in London and many ladies, though accustomed to wash their hands and faces daily, neglect washing their bodies from year to year.'
(A doctor, in 1801)

Bathroom Revolution

Jean-Paul Marat's life and death were strangely linked to the bath. Marat wrote a newspaper which helped to inspire the French Revolution. He was then forced to hide from his enemies in the Paris sewers. Here he caught a painful skin disease, which meant he could only write from the comfort of his bath. In 1793, Marat was assassinated by a woman named Charlotte Corday. She stabbed him while he was taking a bath.

▲ The death of Jean-Paul Marat in his bath.

Salty Dips

The 1700s were a great age for spa towns such as Bath, Buxton and Harrogate. Lavish public baths were built in these towns, where people could drink and swim in mineral water to cure their ailments. Sea-water bathing was also popular, either in the sea or in hot salt-water baths on the shore. People even drank sea water from Brighton, which was bottled up for sale in London.

▼ Brighton bathers hop into the sea from wheeled huts called bathing machines.

Bathing Business

Clean and Decent

The Victorians believed that you had to be clean to be respectable. But few houses had bathrooms like we have today, with water piped to fitted baths. Instead, portable baths were filled up and used anywhere in the house. Poorer people bathed by the kitchen fire. In larger homes, maids had to carry the bath and the water upstairs.

▼ This Victorian bath has the luxury of a single, cold tap in the shape of a swan's head.

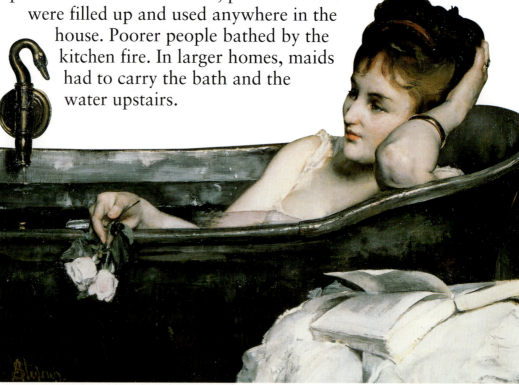

Water Lily

Early soaps were harmful to the skin. So when Andrew Pears began to make a gentle, perfumed soap, he was sure of success. Pears persuaded a beautiful actress called Lily Langtry to appear in advertisements saying: 'For years I have used your soap, and no other.' At last it was safe to have a good scrub.

▶ A famous Victorian advertisement for Pears soap.

24

Clean Profits

Soap-makers were not the only ones to make clean profits from the bathing industry. Seaside resorts and the new railways made money from the many travelling bathers. Meanwhile, factories produced catalogues of bathroom items such as plugs, taps, soap dishes, sponge rests, towel rails and bathside cigar holders. One manufacturer's catalogue told bathers: 'A cold bath is one of the most refreshing comforts and luxuries of life ... calculated to make the whole body rejoice with buoyancy and exhilaration of spirits.'

FANCY THAT!

Bubble Bath
The actress Cora Pearl was said, in the 1890s, to bathe in champagne. Meanwhile, a ladies' magazine recommended its readers to try wine. Blondes were told to bathe in white wine, brunettes in red.

◀ The slipper bath covered the whole body with the minimum amount of water.

SPEECH BUBBLES

White Wash
The first bath was installed in the White House in Washington, in 1851. It caused an outcry. Americans did not mind their president being clean, but they objected to him enjoying the luxury of a hot bath.

Hips and Slippers

Baths now came in many shapes and sizes. The hip bath (right) was the most common. Sponge baths were shallow bowls to stand in while sponging yourself down. Sitz baths were shaped like chairs, while slipper baths encased the whole body. Doctors recommended a 'wet sheet bath', which involved wrapping the body in a wet sheet and shivering until dry. Brrr!

▶ A Victorian hip bath. Notice the soap dishes on the sides.

Turn of the Tap

Hot and Cold

From the 1880s, builders often included plumbing in new houses. Running water now inspired new bathroom inventions. One hot idea was the General Gordon gas bath, which had a naked flame beneath it to heat the bath. A cooler invention was the high-powered shower-bath. One poor man ran his new shower-bath so cold that he was stabbed in the back by a falling icicle.

◄ Thomas Crapper's hooded bath combined a shower with a bath. It cost over £35, about £5,000 at today's values.

Moving Stories

Inventors also turned their minds to keeping clean while on the move. Foldaway 'sponge-baths' were invented for use by travelling holidaymakers. A bathroom was installed in Queen Victoria's new train. A complete, cast-iron bathroom was also taken to the Boer War by General Buller of the British Army. The strain of transporting it through the African heat seriously held up his army's progress!

SPEECH BUBBLES

Bathroom Blues
A Victorian lady plumber called Shirley Murphy recommended daily cold baths, but warned: 'If the skin turns blue, the practice must be given up.'

◄ The washbasin from Queen Victoria's rooms on the 1869 royal train.

◄ *Ophelia*, painted by Sir John Millais. In Shakespeare's play *Hamlet*, Ophelia goes mad and drowns after her father is murdered by Hamlet.

Water Colours

Nudes have always been popular subjects for artists. What better place to paint them than in the bath? The French painter Pierre Bonnard's model was his wife. She spent hours in the bath to ease a skin complaint, so that is where he painted her. When the English artist Sir John Millais painted the drowned Ophelia, he used a model called Lizzie Siddell. Because Lizzie had to pose for so long, Millais kept the water warm with hot lamps under the bath.

Cold Comfort

In 1846, parliament said that towns should provide free baths for the poor. Baths were becoming available to all, but water tanks and pipes could be more trouble than they were worth. In winter, they froze and burst. Early hot water systems also tended to overheat and explode. Until the early 1900s, most baths still had just the one tap, marked 'cold'.

► Washing facilities were provided for the poor at this London shelter in 1870.

FANCY THAT!

Marble Marvel
In 1837, Queen Victoria had the huge marble bath at Brighton Pavilion broken up. She then had it made into mantelpieces for Buckingham Palace.

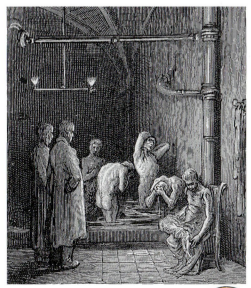

Water Wars

Coal Comfort

After the 1920s, baths were put into most new houses. Some people thought them a waste of space. Instead of washing themselves in the bath, they kept the coal in it. Gradually, however, the bathing habit caught on.

Having a bath was no longer considered 'posh'. It was something everyone could enjoy. The cleaner people became, the more they noticed the odours of their unwashed friends. For most of us, a regular bath is no longer a luxury. It is a necessity.

► Until the 1940s, many people like this miner in Wales still used a tin bath in front of the fire.

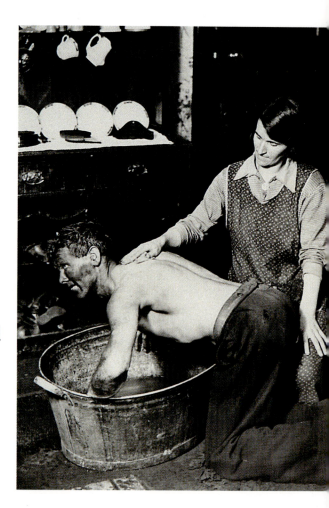

Bath Assaults

The bathroom became one of the most dangerous rooms in the house. An investigation in the 1930s found that at least 10,000 people were injured or killed in bathroom accidents every year. Some victims had slipped or drowned in the bath. Others had been poisoned by gas, burnt or electrocuted.

FANCY THAT!

Clean as Mustard
In the 1930s, Colman's the mustard makers started the Mustard Club. Instead of using bath salts or bubble bath, members of the club added mustard powder to their bathwater. This was said to be good for colds and skin complaints. It gives a whole new meaning to a 'hot bath'.

Winston's Waste

During the Second World War, there was often barely enough fuel to keep warm and cook food. Heating up the bathwater seemed wasteful, so baths were strictly rationed in most homes. To save water, the government asked people to paint a black line round the bath at the depth of five inches (13 cm). The bath was never to be filled above this level. Many people wondered if Winston Churchill, the Prime Minister, obeyed this rule. He was, after all, quite large around the waist!

Chocolate Whirls

The days of simple body-shaped tubs are over. Many homes now have corner baths, round baths, or sunken baths built for two or more people. Some bathrooms have whirlpools, jacuzzis or saunas. You do not even have to fill the bath with water these days. In 1996, an American couple were married in their bathroom while bathing in hot chocolate.

▲ A wartime poster which encouraged people to save fuel.

Speech Bubbles

A Tight Squeeze
A survey of modern bathrooms found 'lavatory seats too high, washbasins too small, baths too cramped and dangerous, showers too awkward and most fixtures unsightly, insanitary and not well adapted to the human form'. (*Bathrooms*, by Mary Gilliat)

◀ This modern bathroom has its walls, shower and bath all made from stainless steel.

BATH TIMES

2500 BC	Bathrooms and drains are built at Mohenjo-Daro, India.
1450 BC	The Royal Palace at Knossos, Crete, has a splendid bathroom.
1350 BC	An Egyptian house at Tel-el-Amarna has a bathroom and shallow bath.
AD c. 350	Mixed bathing allowed in public baths in Rome.
c. 540	St Benedict says monks must bathe only rarely.
745	St Boniface forbids mixed bathing.
900	Vikings are recorded washing every day.
1326	Hot spring baths open at the town of Spa in France.
1351	King Edward III installs hot and cold water taps in his bathroom.
1449	The bishop orders bathers at Bath to wear costumes.
1480s	Turkish baths become popular in London.
1560s	Queen Elizabeth I takes a monthly bath.
1651	The first English reference to a toothbrush.
1680	The first recorded bath made from copper.
1712	The bidet is invented in France.
1846	*The Public Baths and Wash Houses Act* orders towns to provide baths for the poor.
1851	The Great Exhibition includes 727 exhibits by soap-makers. The first 'en suite' bathrooms, Mount Vernon Hotel, New Jersey, USA.
1853	Prime Minister William Gladstone ends the tax on soap.
1862	Andrew Pears builds the first large soap factory.
1868	Benjamin Waddy Maughan invents the gas geyser water heater.
1930s	Colman's 'Mustard Club' encourages mustard baths. 10,000 people are injured every year in their bathrooms.
1940s	Water rationing limits depth of bathwater to 13 cm.
1967	The first plastic bathroom suites are made by Habitat.
1998	A report says that businessmen do their most useful thinking in the bath.

ROOMS TO VISIT

Chatsworth House, Chatsworth, Derbyshire. Tel: 01246 582204
Georgian marble baths and the famous grotto.

Chedworth Roman Villa, Chedworth, Cirencester, Gloucestershire. Tel: 01242 890256
A Roman villa with bathroom suite and hypocaust.

Gladstone Pottery Museum, Stoke-on-Trent, Staffordshire. Tel: 01782 319232
Victorian baths, bathroom suites and WCs galore.

National Railway Museum, Leeman Road, York, Yorkshire. Tel: 01904 621261
The private bathrooms of the royal trains.

Osborne House, East Cowes, Isle of Wight. Tel: 01983 200022
Queen Victoria's bathroom in the house designed by her husband, Prince Albert.

Roman Baths Museum, Pump Room, Bath, Somerset. Tel: 01225 477000
Roman baths with hot spring baths still functioning.

GLOSSARY

ablutions	Washing of the body.
anointers	People who 'anoint', or apply, oil or ointment.
appliances	Pieces of household equipment.
aquamanile	A type of jug used for pouring water for washing one's hands.
brunettes	Women with dark or brown hair.
cauliflower ears	Ears swollen by many blows, especially from boxing.
conduit	A channel or pipe for carrying liquids.
despised	Disliked, looked down on.
fjords	Long, narrow streams of water coming from the sea, especially in Scandinavia.
font	The bath in a church which contains water for baptism.
founder	A worker who makes things by melting and moulding metal.
grotto	A room made to look like a cave.
hereafter	In the future.
hip bath	A small, portable bath in which a bather sits.
jacuzzi	A bath with underwater jets of water to massage the body.
jousts	Contests between two knights with lances, on horseback.
leprosy	A disease which damages the skin and nerves.
mallow	A plant with hairy stems and leaves.
manicure	Treatment for the hands and nails.
monasteries	Buildings where monks live.
mosaic	A picture created from many small pieces of glass or stone.
necessity	Something that must be done.
nosegays	Bunches of sweet-smelling flowers.
oaf	A fool, idiot.
Pharaoh	A ruler of ancient Egypt.
Phoenician	Of an ancient people who lived in Phoenicia, where Syria and Lebanon are today.
pillaged	Plundered and stole goods during war.
pocks	Pockmarks: small pus-filled spots on the skin.
pomanders	Balls of perfume carried in boxes or bags.
resolution	An oath or promise to do something.
sanitation	The removal of sewage and rubbish from homes.
sauna	A room heated to a high temperature to cleanse the body.
sinful	Bad or wicked.
squires	Knights' attendants, who were training to be knights.
strigil	A metal scraper for scraping oil off the body.
terracotta	A type of pottery.
vapours	Depression, thought to be caused by vapours from the stomach.

BATHTIME READING

Clean and Decent by L. Wright (RKP, 1971)
Keeping Clean, A Very Peculiar History by D. Kerr (Watts, 1995)
Medieval Muck, Smelly Old History by Mary Dobson (Oxford, 1999)
Reeking Royals, Smelly Old History by Mary Dobson (Oxford, 1999)
The Book of the Bath by C. Kanner (Piatkus Books, 1986)
The Victorian Bathroom Catalogue by K. Wedd (Studio Editions, Random House, 1996)